EASY PIANO

CHART HITS
of 2012-2013

ISBN 978-1-4803-3797-8

HAL•LEONARD®
CORPORATION

7777 W. BLUEMOUND RD. P.O. BOX 13819 MILWAUKEE, WI 53213

Visit Hal Leonard Online at
www.halleonard.com

THE A TEAM

Words and Music by
ED SHEERAN

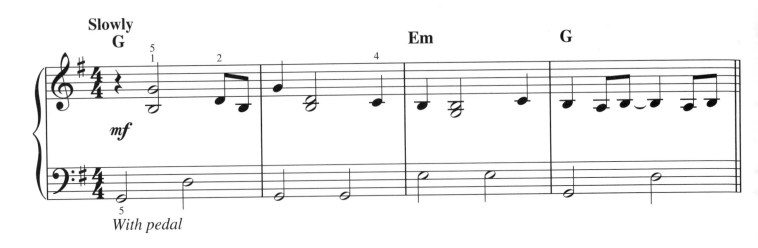

White lips, ___ pale face, ___ breath - ing in snow -
Ripped gloves, ___ rain - coat, ___ tried to swim, stay a -

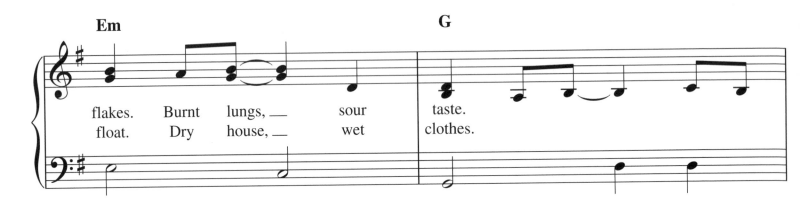

flakes. Burnt lungs, ___ sour taste.
float. Dry house, ___ wet clothes.

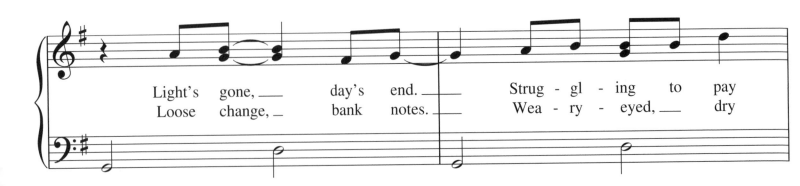

Light's gone, ___ day's end. ___ Strug - gl - ing to pay
Loose change, ___ bank notes. ___ Wea - ry - eyed, ___ dry

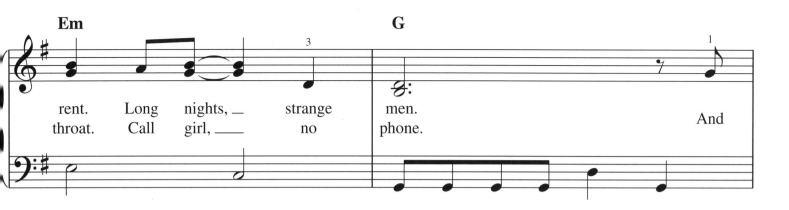

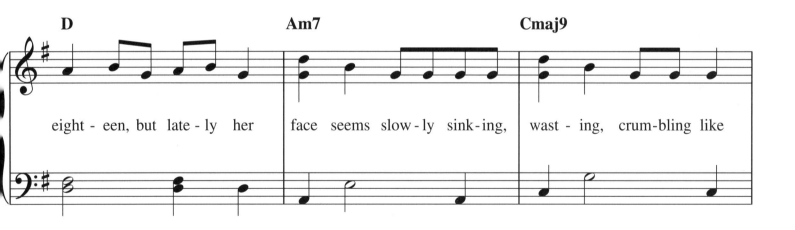

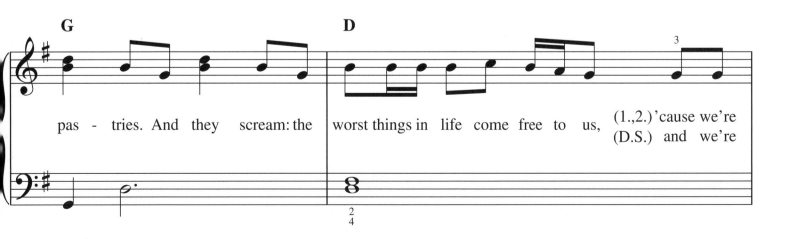

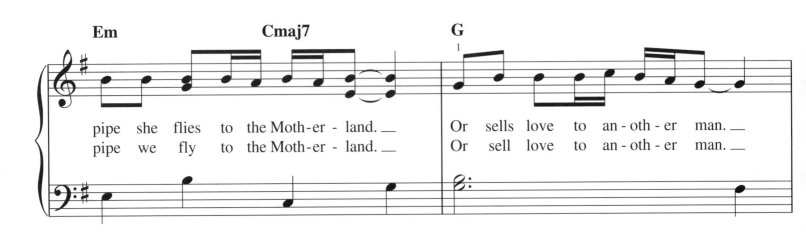

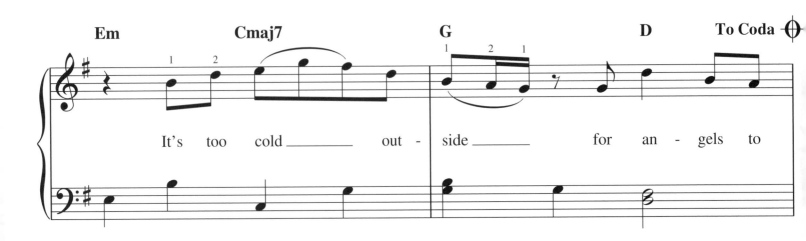

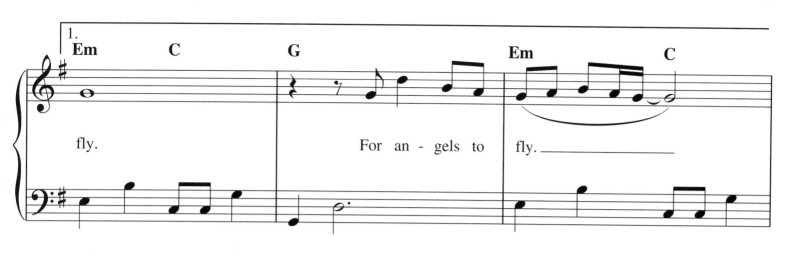

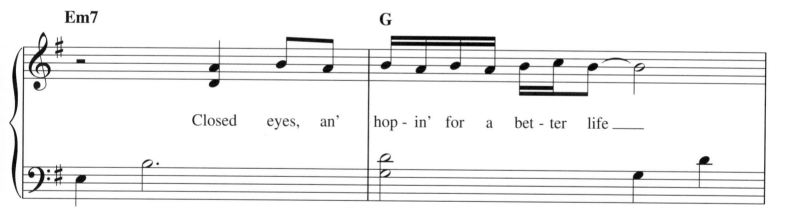

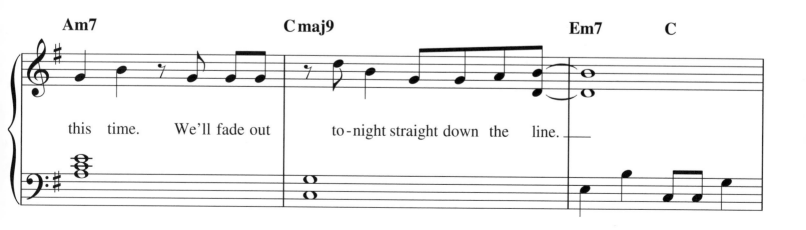

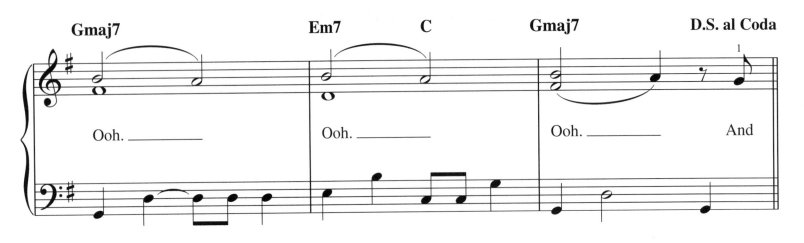

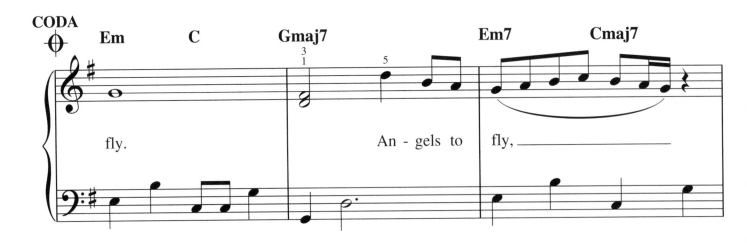

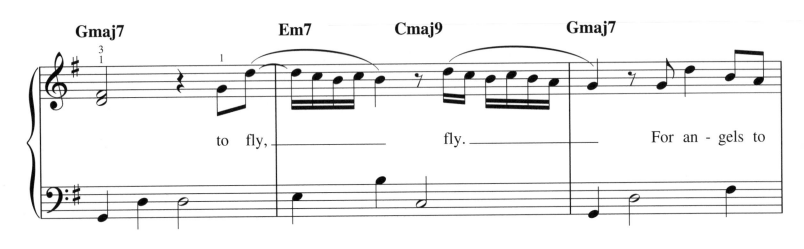

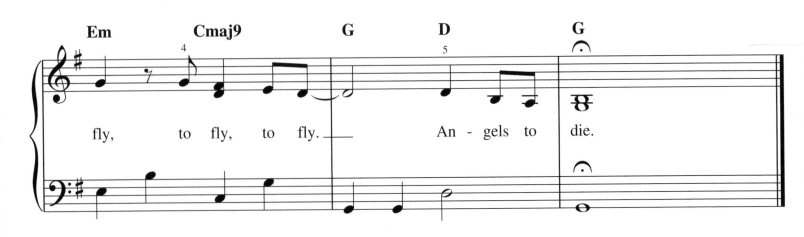

I WON'T GIVE UP

Words and Music by JASON MRAZ
and MICHAEL NATTER

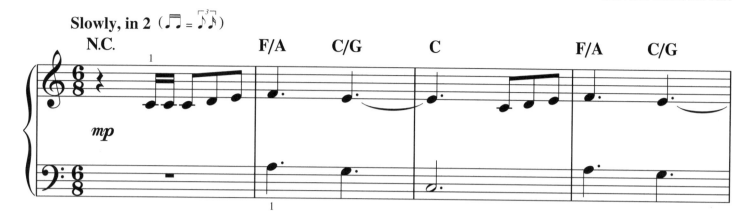

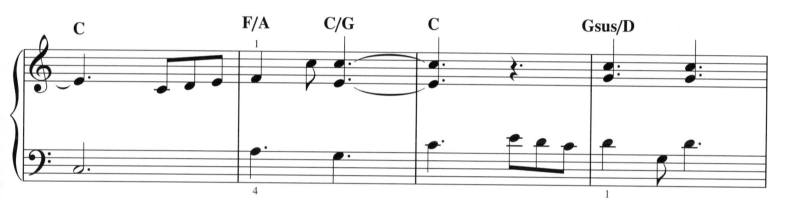

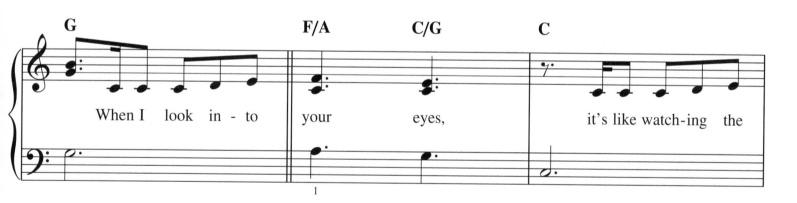

When I look in-to your eyes, it's like watch-ing the

night sky or a beau-ti-ful sun - rise.

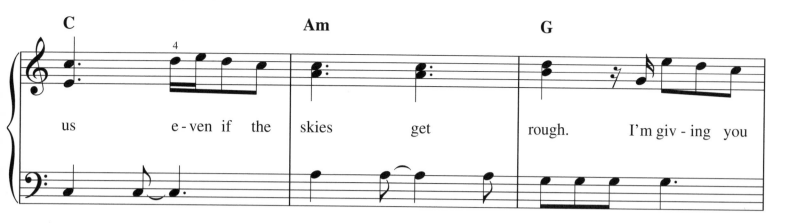

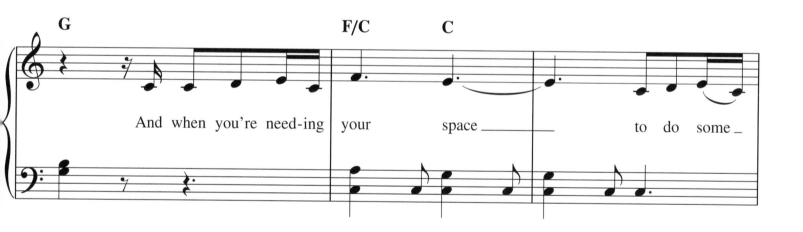

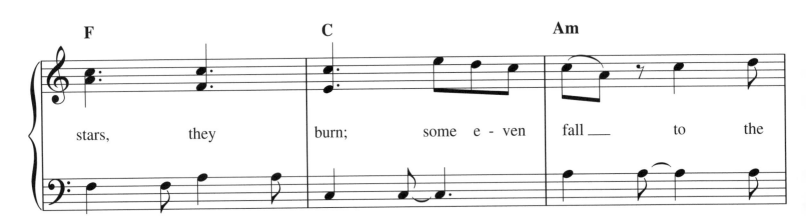

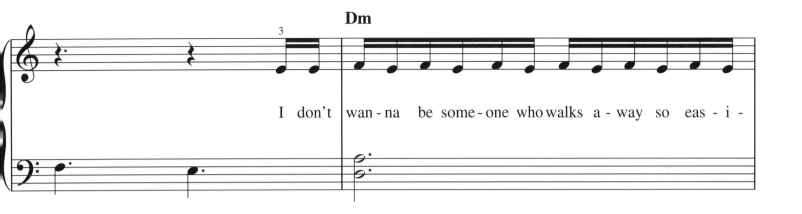

I don't wan-na be some-one who walks a-way so eas-i-

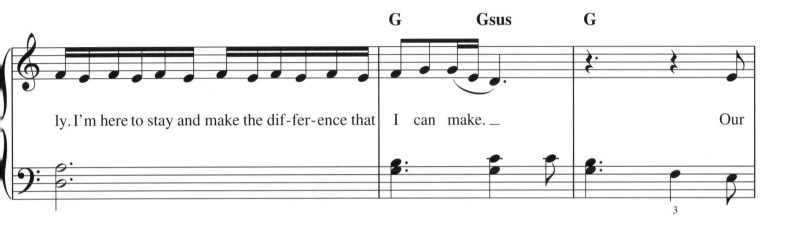

ly. I'm here to stay and make the dif-fer-ence that I can make. ___ Our

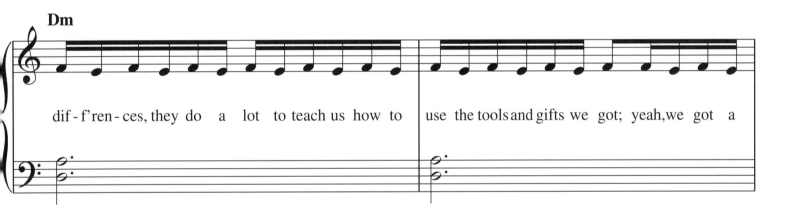

dif-f'ren-ces, they do a lot to teach us how to use the tools and gifts we got; yeah, we got a

lot at stake. ___ And in the end, you're still my friend; at least we did in-tend for

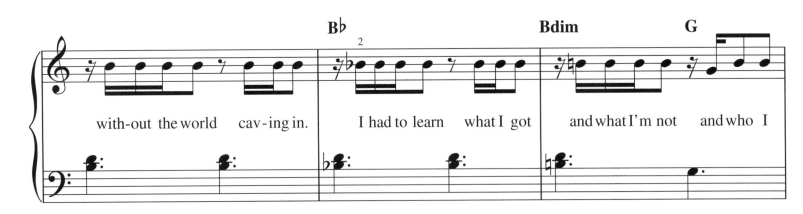

AS LONG AS YOU LOVE ME

Words and Music by JUSTIN BIEBER,
SEAN ANDERSON, NASRI ATWEH,
RODNEY JERKINS and ANDRE LINDAL

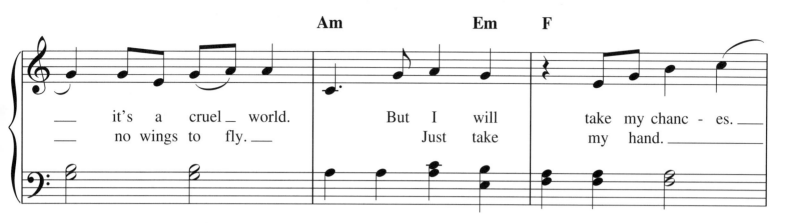

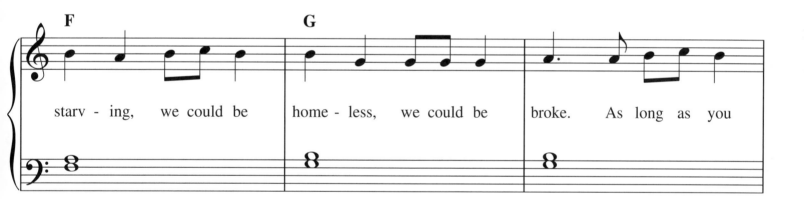

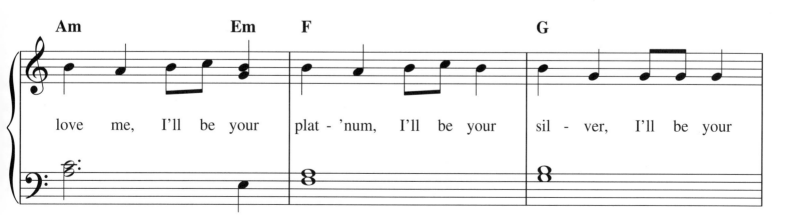

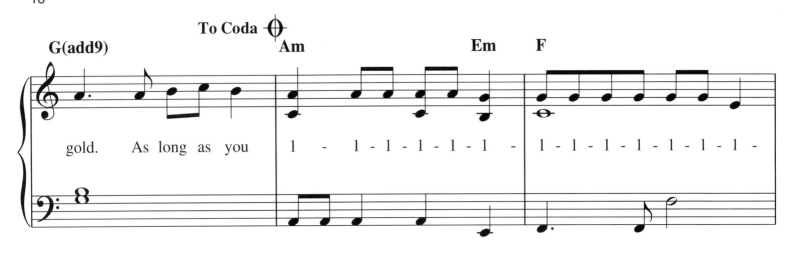

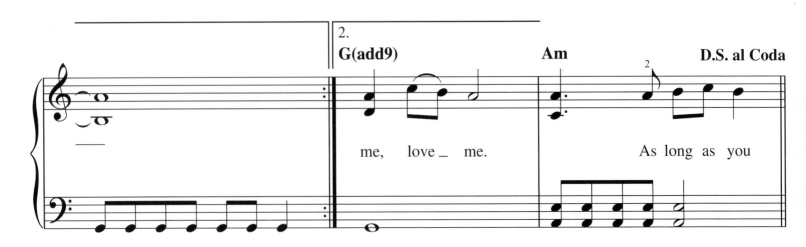

BLOW ME
(One Last Kiss)

Words and Music by ALECIA MOORE
and GREG KURSTIN

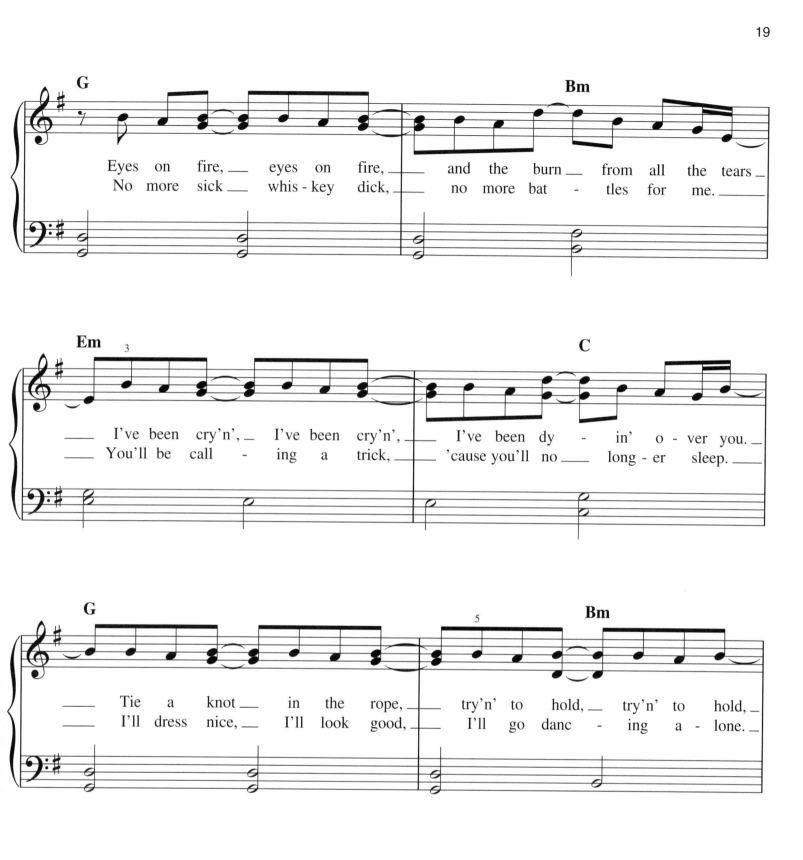

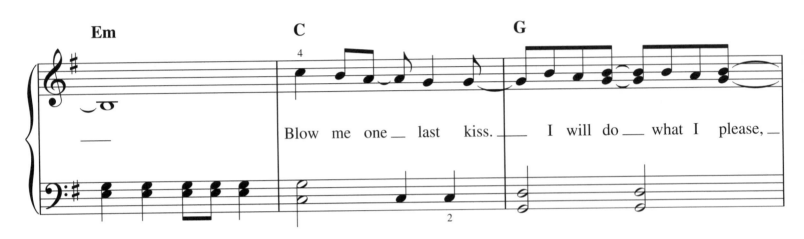

50 WAYS TO SAY GOODBYE

Words and Music by PAT MONAHAN,
ESPEN LIND and AMUND BJORKLUND

Moderate groove, in Mariachi style

My heart is
My pride still

par - a - lyzed,
feels the sting,

my head was
you were my

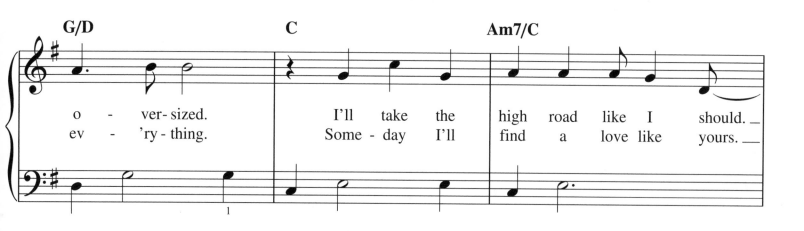

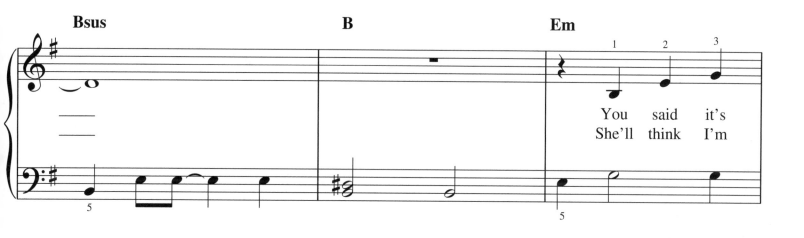

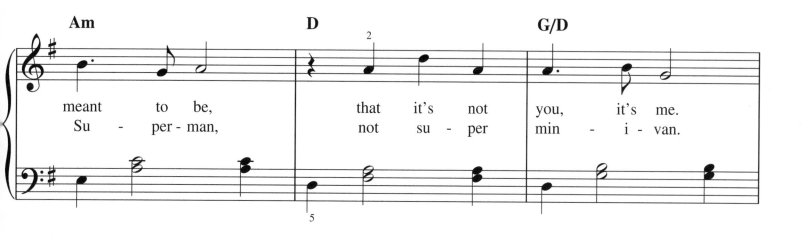

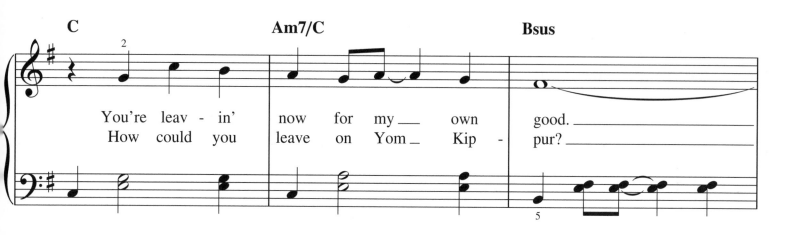

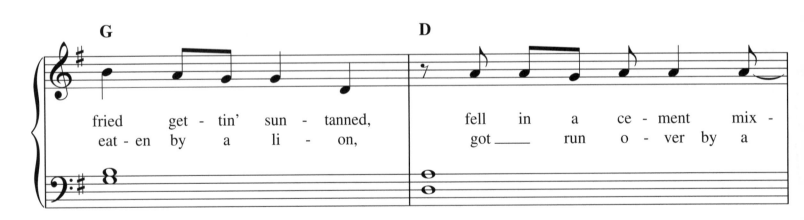

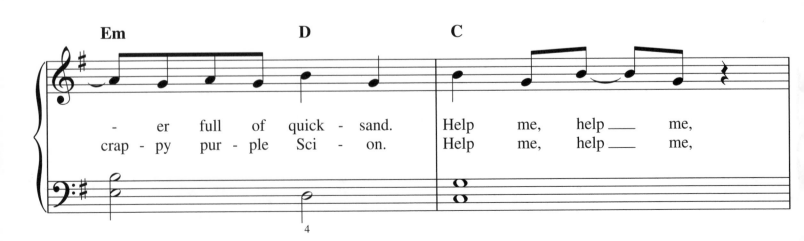

I'm no good __ at good - byes. __
I'm no good __ at good - byes. __

She met a shark un - der wa - ter, fell and no one caught her.
She __ dried up in the des - ert, drowned in a hot tub,

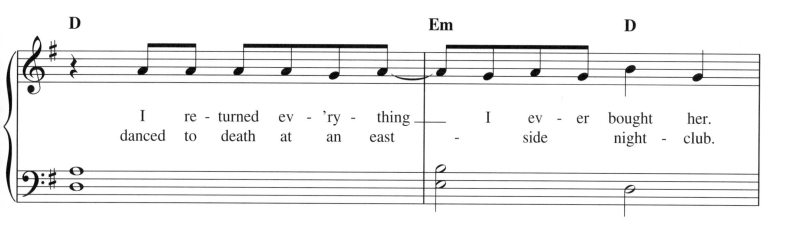

I re - turned ev - 'ry - thing __ I ev - er bought her.
danced to death at an east - side night - club.

Help me, help __ me, I'm all out __ of lies and

28

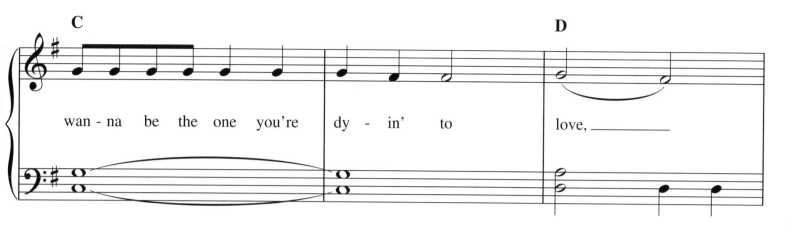

wan - na be the one you're dy - in' to love, _____

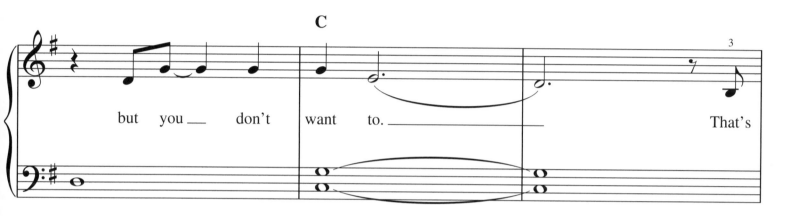

but you __ don't want to. _____ That's

cool, but if my friends ask where you are I'm gon - na say, that's

cool, but if my friends ask where you are I'm gon - na say: She went

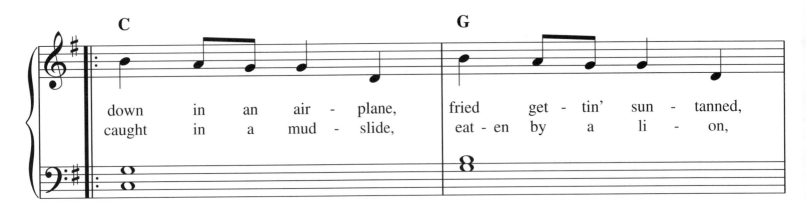

down in an air - plane,
caught in a mud - slide,

fried get - tin' sun - tanned,
eat - en by a li - on,

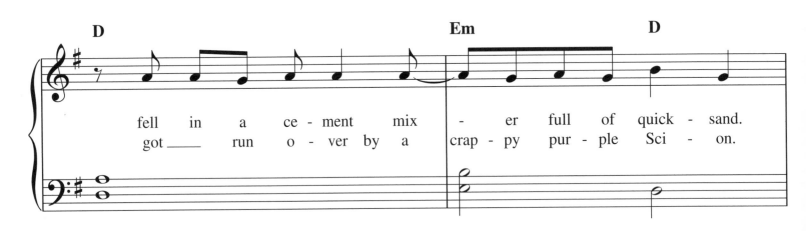

fell in a ce - ment mix
got ___ run o - ver by a

- er full of quick - sand.
crap - py pur - ple Sci - on.

Help me, help ___ me,
Help me, help ___ me,

I'm no good ___ at good - byes. ___
I'm no good ___ at good - byes. ___

___
___

She met a shark un - der wa - ter,
She ___ dried up in the des - ert,

fell and no one caught her.
drowned ___ in a hot tub,

I re - turned ev - 'ry - thing ___
danced to death at an east -

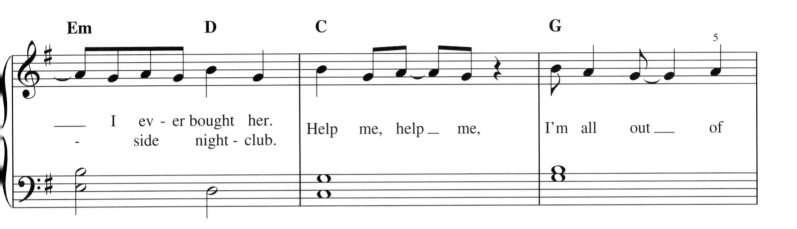

___ I ev - er bought her.
- side night - club.

Help me, help ___ me,

I'm all out ___ of

lies.

She was

lies,

and ways to say ___ you

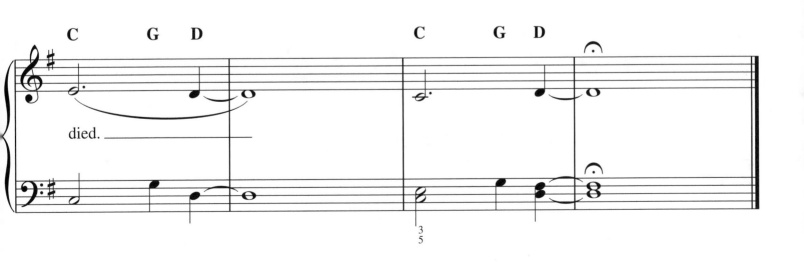

died. _____

HO HEY

Words and Music by JEREMY FRAITES
and WESLEY SCHULTZ

Moderately, in two

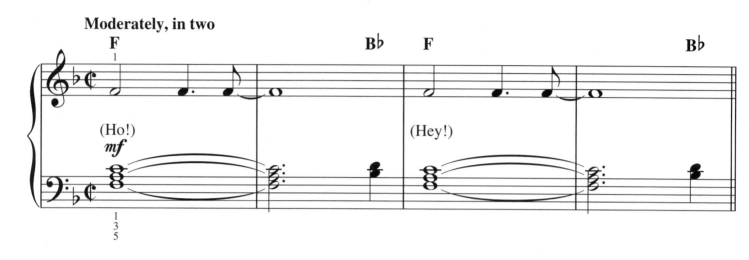

(Ho!)

mf

(Hey!)

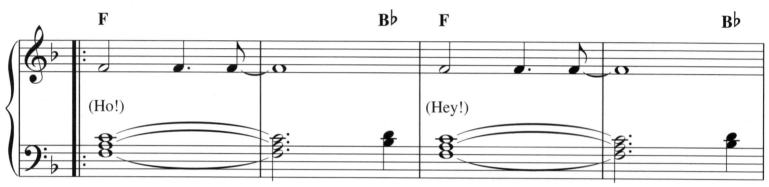

(Ho!)

(Hey!)

(Ho!)   I've been try'n' to do   it right;
(Ho!)   So   show me, fam - i - ly,

(Hey!)   I've been liv-in' a lone - ly life. _____
(Hey!)   all the blood _____ that I _____ will bleed. _____

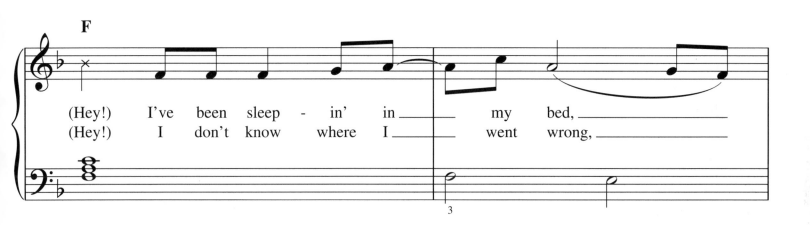

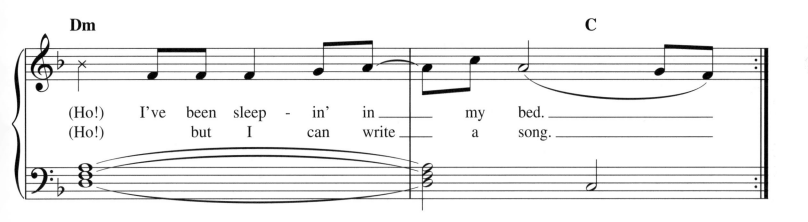

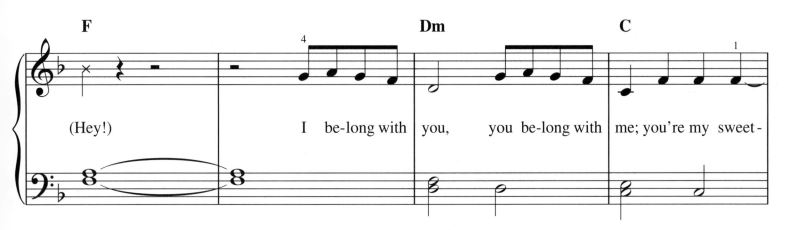

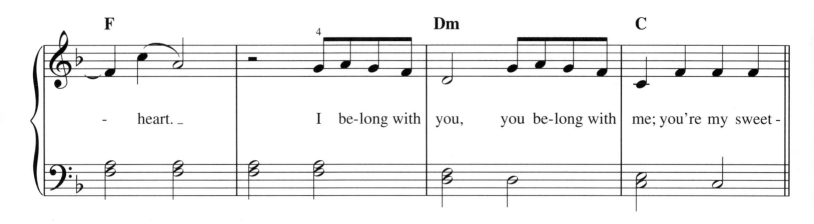

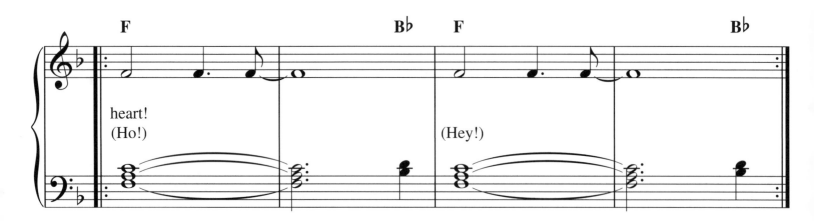

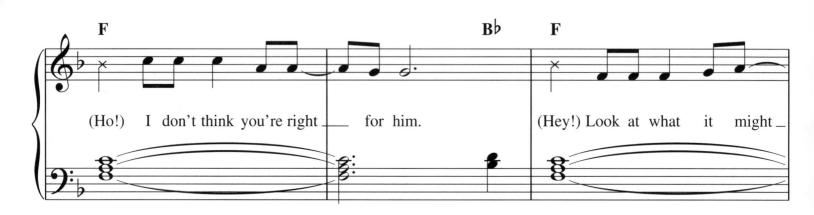

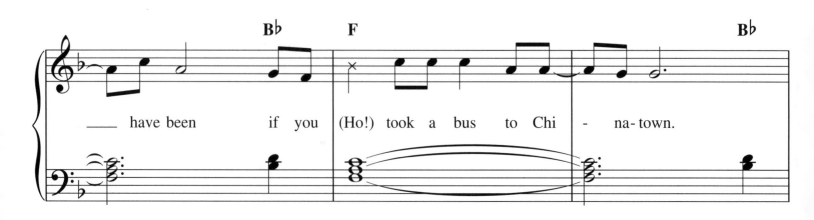

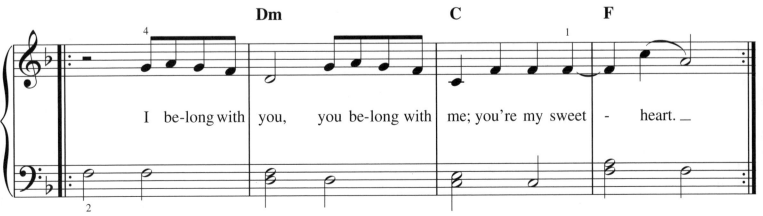

36

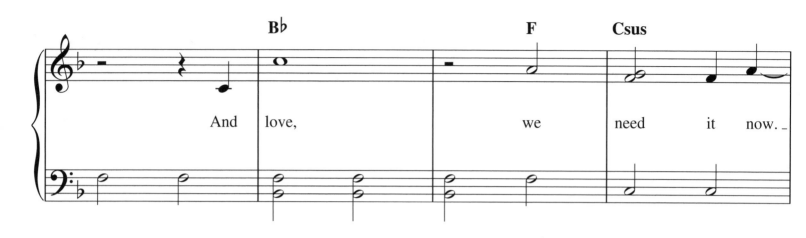

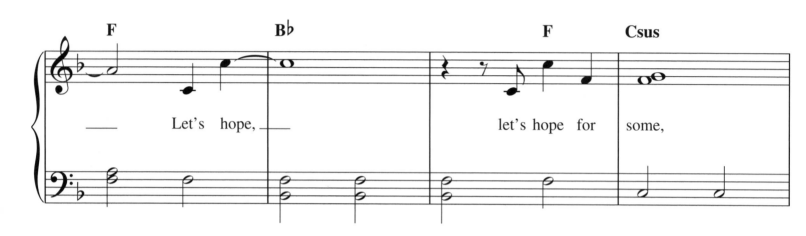

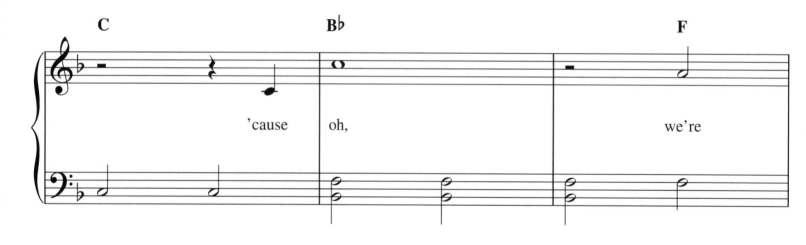

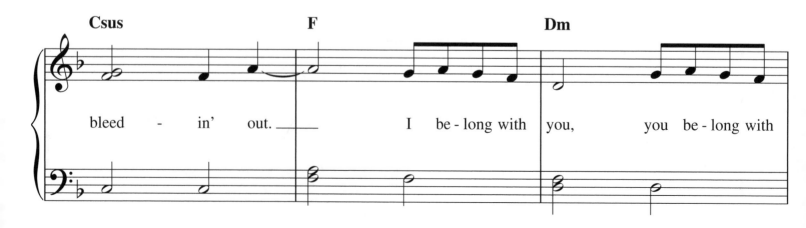

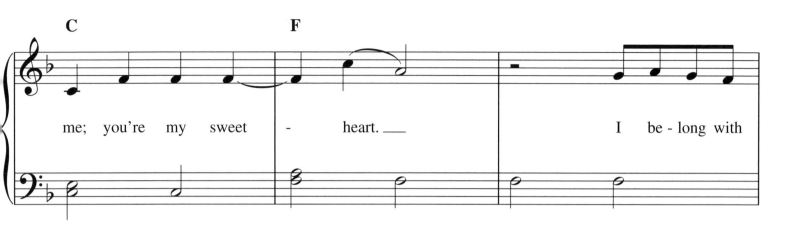

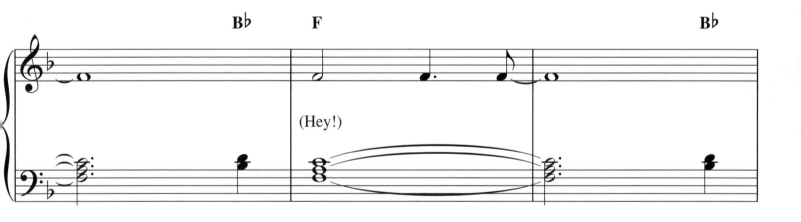

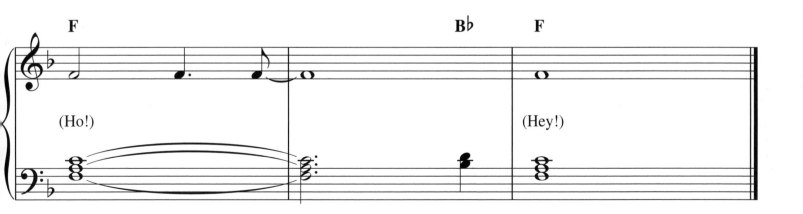

I KNEW YOU WERE TROUBLE.

Words and Music by TAYLOR SWIFT,
SHELLBACK and MAX MARTIN

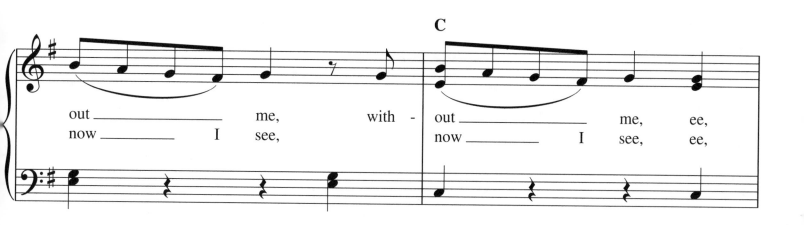

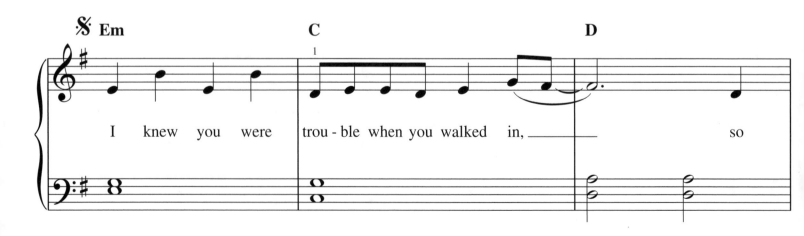

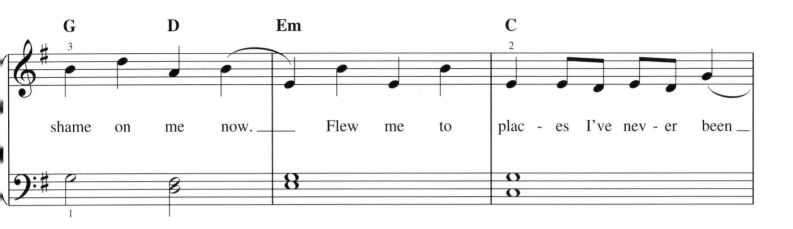

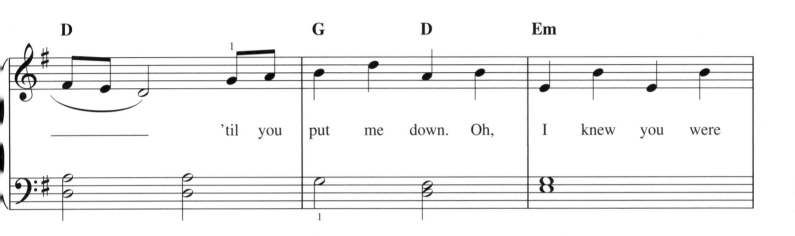

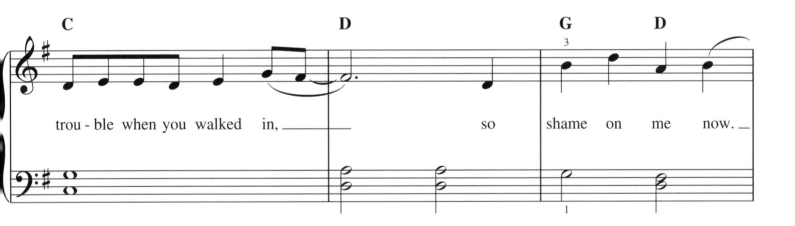

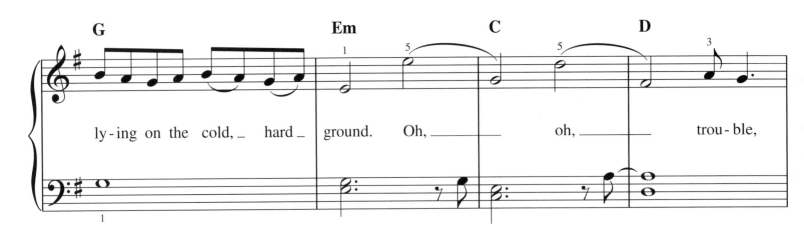

ly-ing on the cold, _ hard _ ground.   Oh, _____   oh, _____   trou-ble,

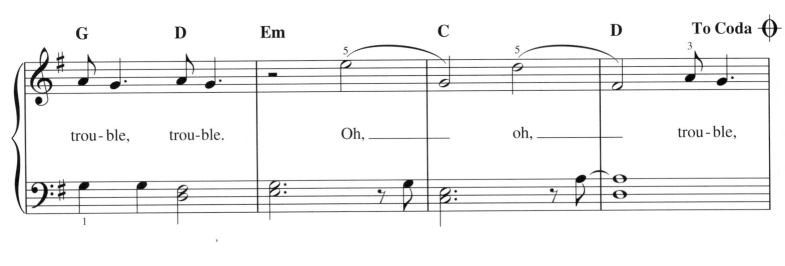

trou-ble,   trou-ble.   Oh, _____   oh, _____   trou-ble,

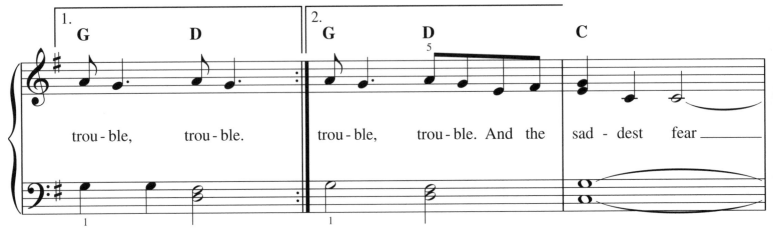

1.
trou-ble,   trou-ble.

2.
trou-ble,   trou-ble. And the   sad-dest   fear _____

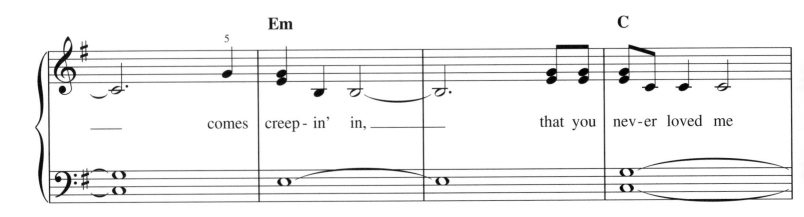

_____   comes creep-in' in, _____   _____   that you nev-er loved me

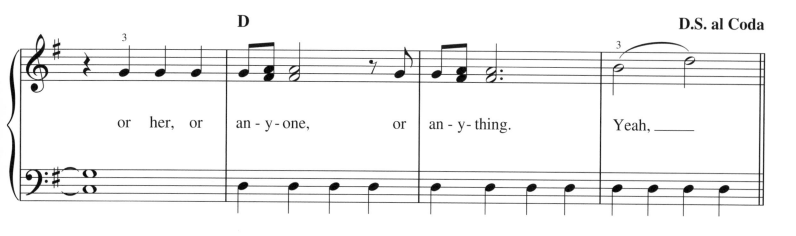

or her, or an-y-one, or an-y-thing. Yeah, ____

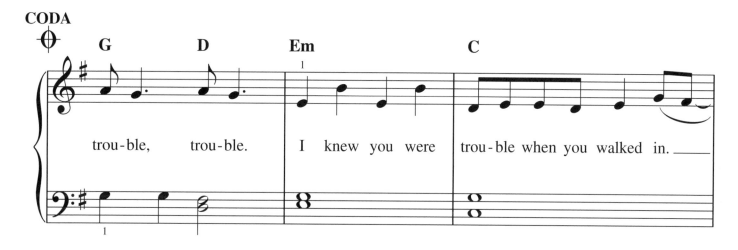

trou-ble, trou-ble. I knew you were trou-ble when you walked in. ____

____ Trou-ble, trou-ble, trou-ble. I knew you were

trou-ble when you walked in. ____ Trou-ble, trou-ble, trou-ble.

IT'S TIME

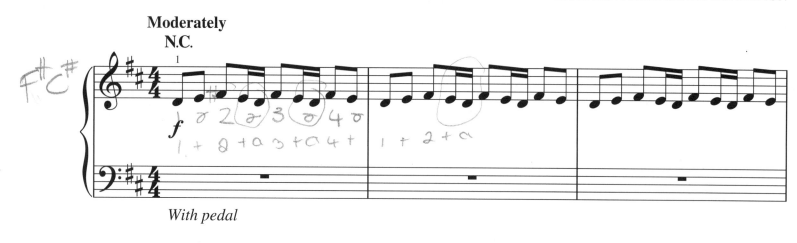

Words and Music by DANIEL REYNOLDS,
BENJAMIN McKEE and DANIEL SERMON

So this is what you meant when you said that you were spent.
this is where you fell, and I am left to sell.

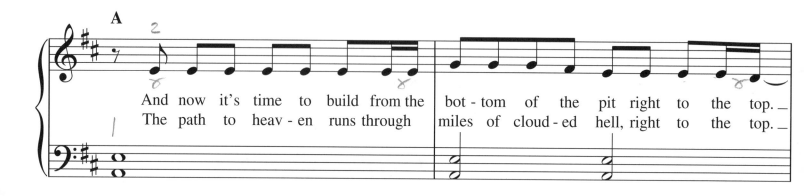

And now it's time to build from the bot-tom of the pit right to the top. _
The path to heav-en runs through miles of cloud-ed hell, right to the top. _

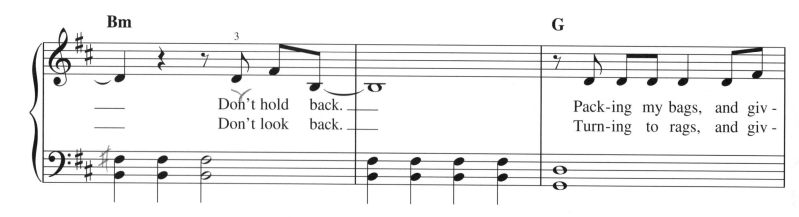

Don't hold back. _ Pack-ing my bags, and giv-
Don't look back. _ Turn-ing to rags, and giv-

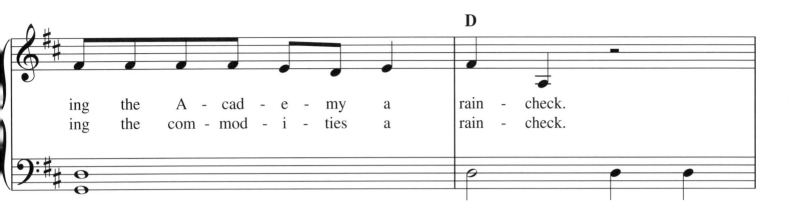

ing the A - cad - e - my a   rain - check.
ing the com - mod - i - ties a   rain - check.

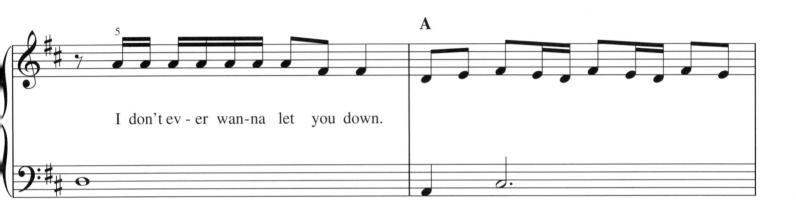

I don't ev - er wan-na let   you down.

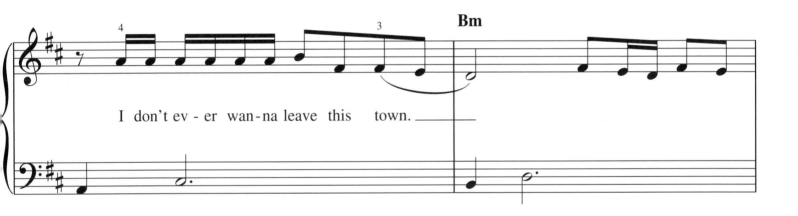

I don't ev - er wan-na leave this   town. _____

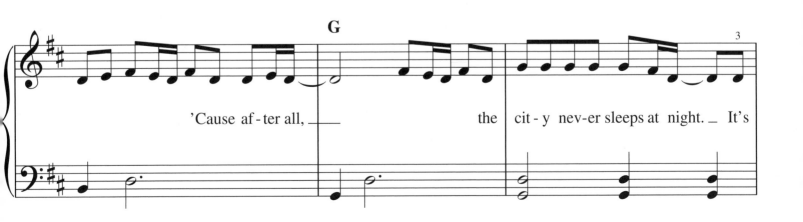

'Cause af - ter all, ____   the   cit - y nev-er sleeps at night. _ It's

time to be - gin, is - n't it? I get a lit - tle bit big - ger, but then, I'll ad - mit,

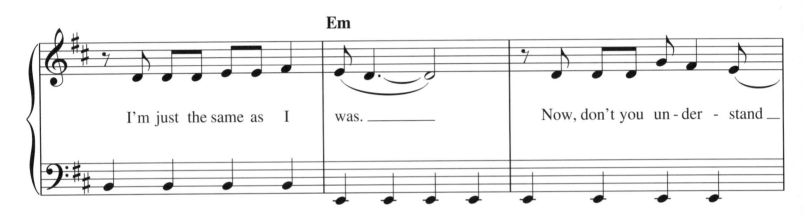

I'm just the same as I was. _____ Now, don't you un - der - stand _

_ that I'm nev - er chang - ing who I am?

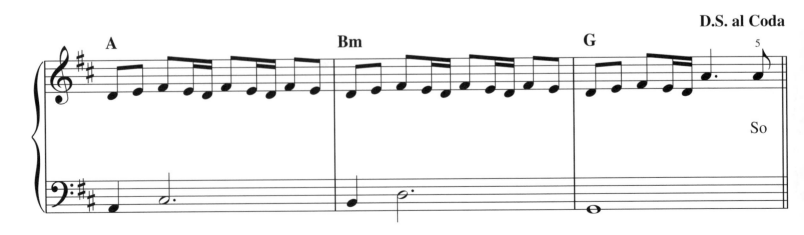

So

CODA

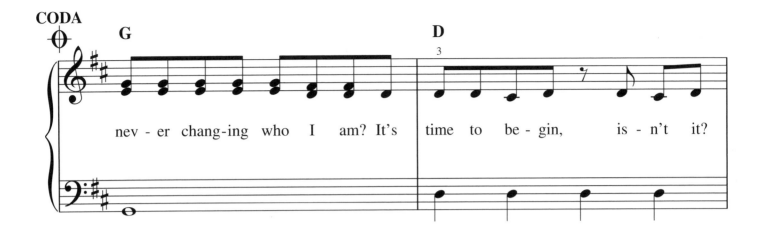

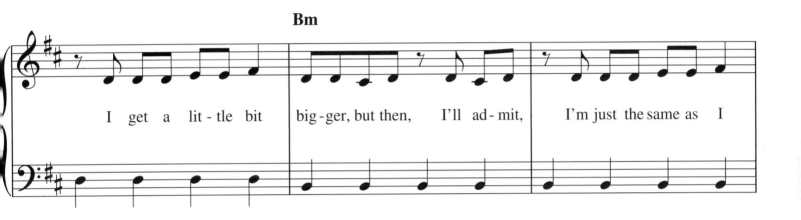

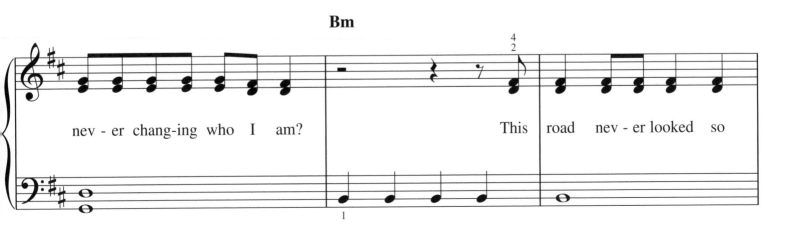

48

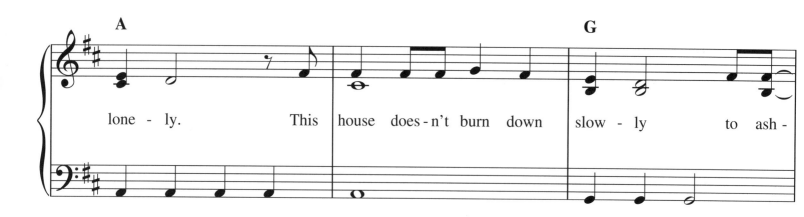

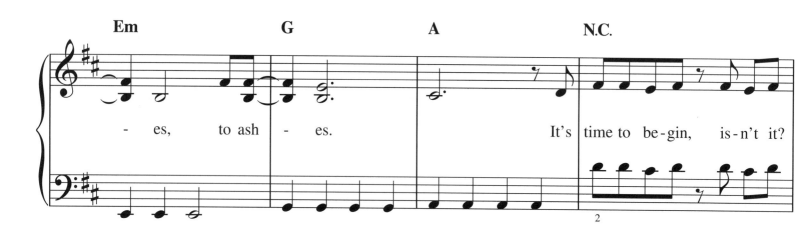

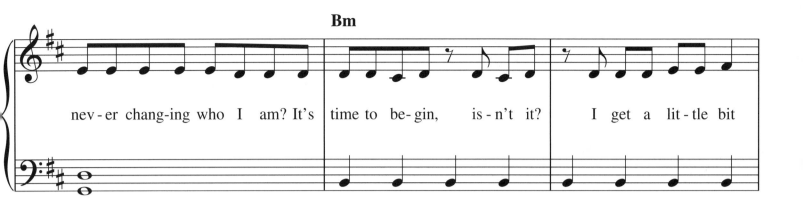

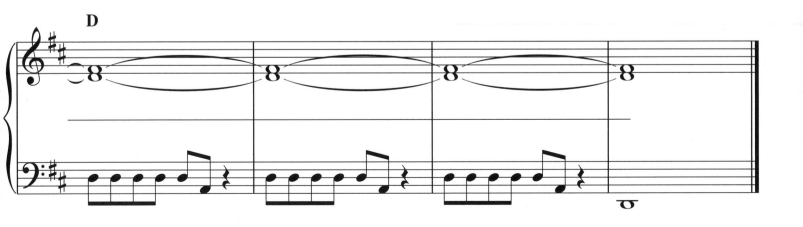

LITTLE TALKS

Words and Music by NANNA HILMARSDOTTIR
and RAGNAR THORHALLSSON

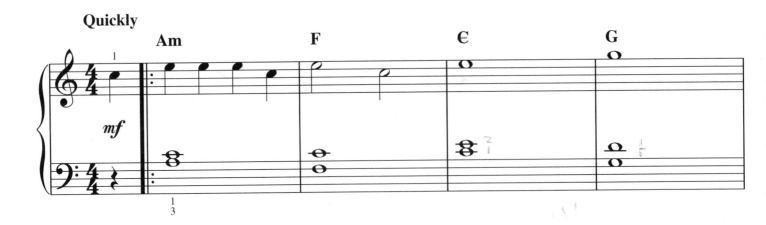

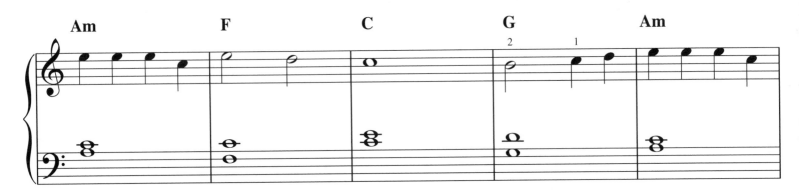

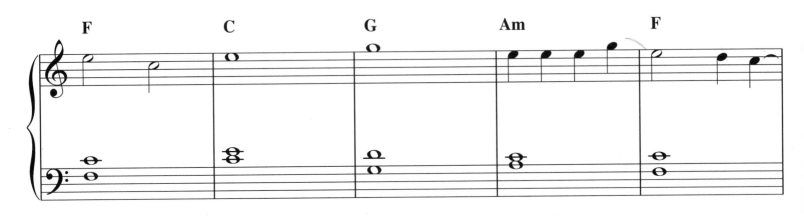

There's an I don't like old____ voice walk-ing a - round____ this in ____ my head ____ that's

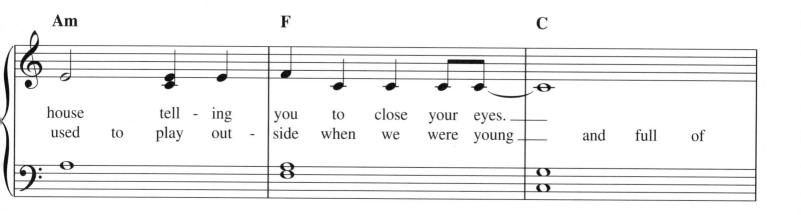

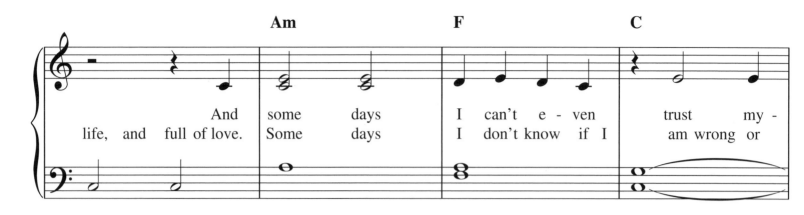

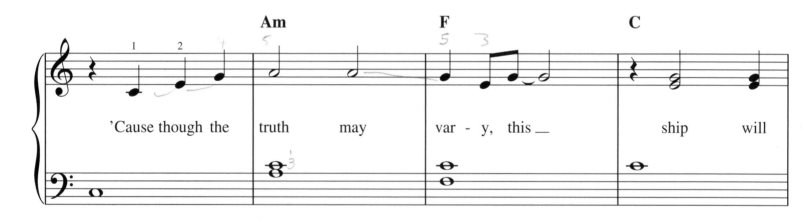

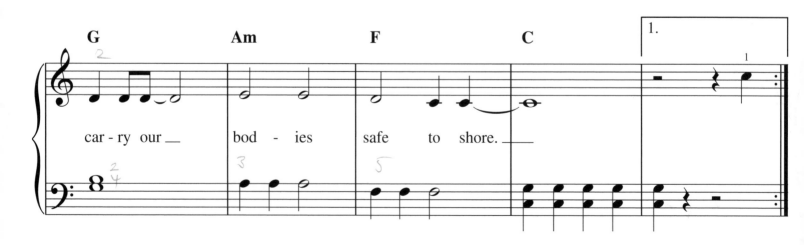

53

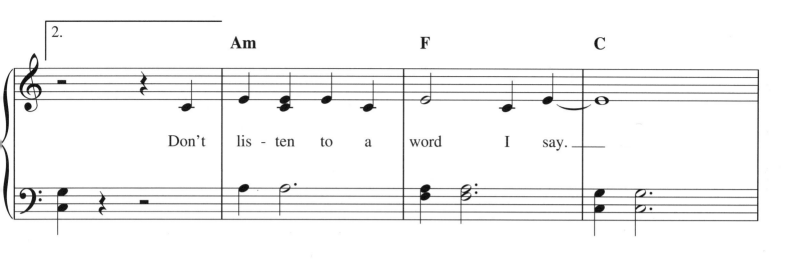

Don't lis - ten to a word I say.

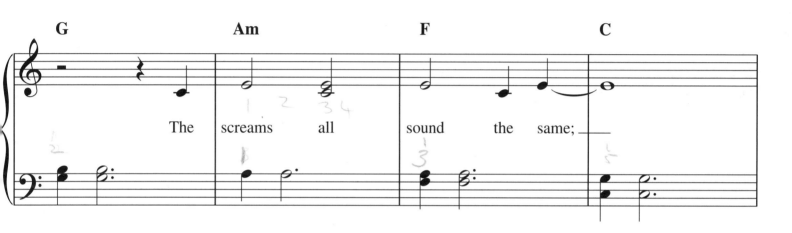

The screams all sound the same;

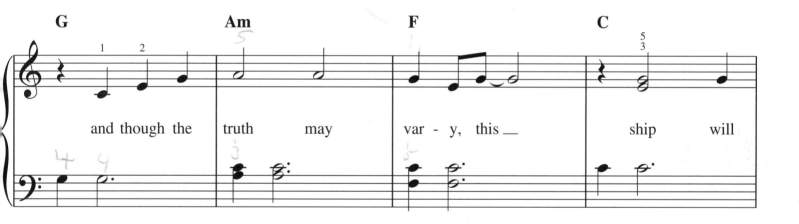

and though the truth may var - y, this ship will

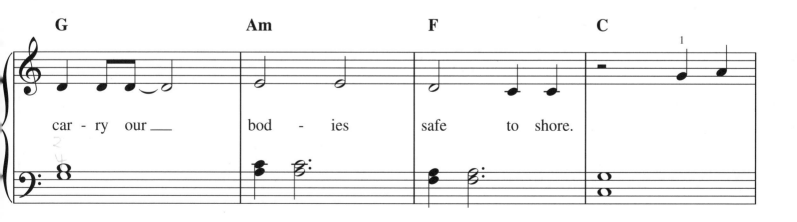

car - ry our bod - ies safe to shore.

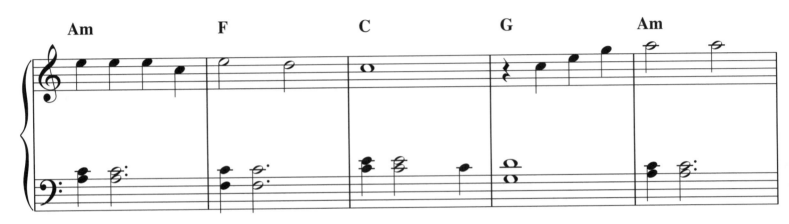

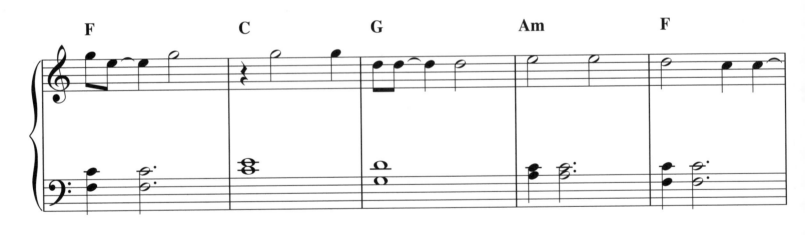

You're

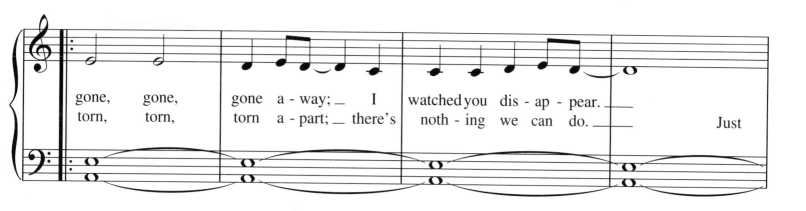

gone, gone, gone a - way; __ I watched you dis - ap - pear. __
torn, torn, torn a - part; __ there's noth - ing we can do. __ Just

All this life is a ghost of you. __
let me go; we'll meet a - gain soon. __

1.

2.

F

Now we're

Now wait, wait, wait for me,

1

C

Am

F

please hang a - round. __ I'll see you when I fall a - sleep. __

LIVE WHILE WE'RE YOUNG

Words and Music by RAMI YACOUB,
SAVAN KOTECHA and CARL FALK

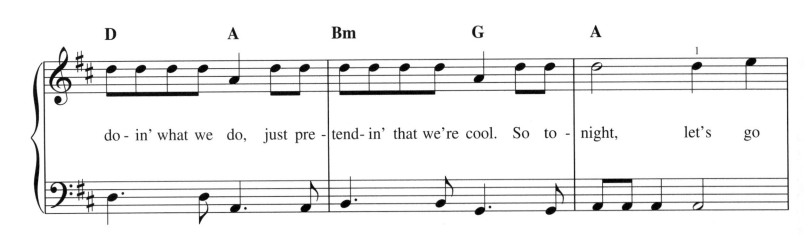

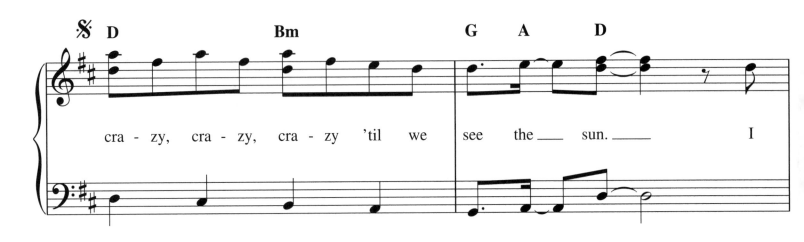

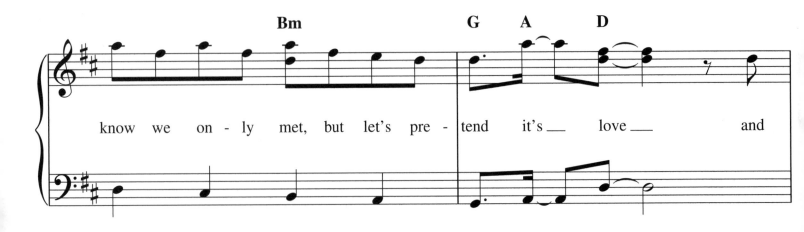

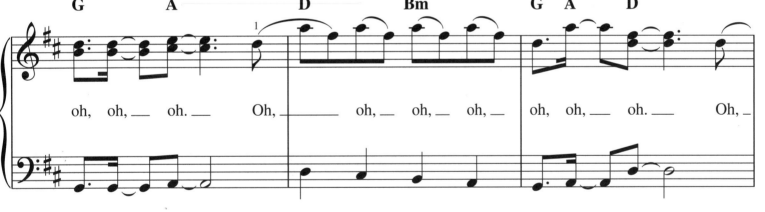

I wan - na live while _ we're young.

We wan - na live while _ we're young. Let's go

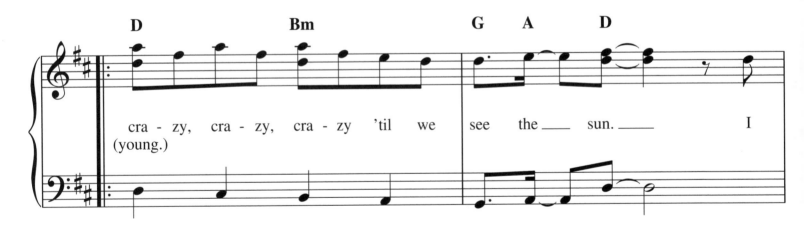

cra - zy, cra - zy, cra - zy 'til we see the __ sun. __ I
(young.)

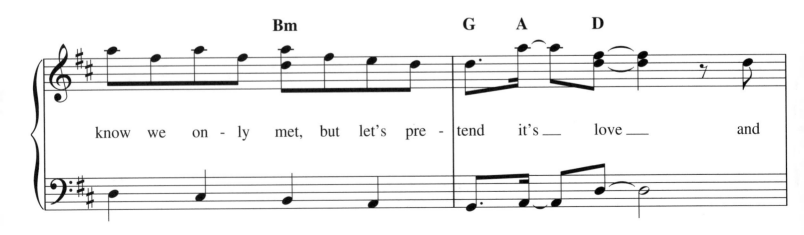

know we on - ly met, but let's pre - tend it's __ love __ and

LOCKED OUT OF HEAVEN

Words and Music by BRUNO MARS,
ARI LEVINE and PHILIP LAWRENCE

But swim-ming in your world ___ is some - thing spir - it - ual; ___
up ___ your ___ gates 'cause I ___ can't wait ___ to see the light. _

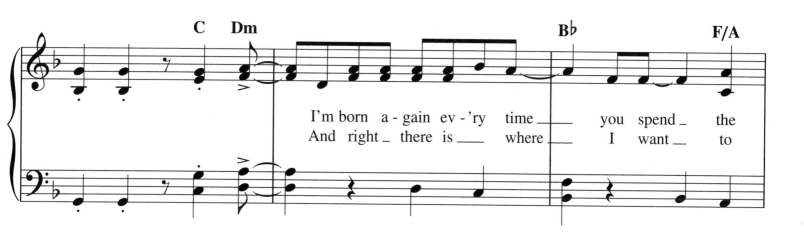

I'm born a - gain ev - 'ry time ___ you spend ___ the
And right _ there is ___ where ___ I want ___ to

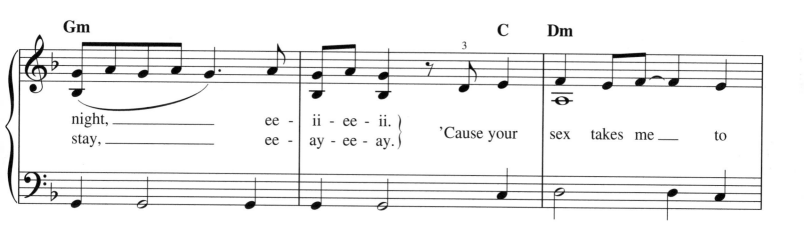

night, _____ ee - ii - ee - ii.
stay, _____ ee - ay - ee - ay. 'Cause your sex takes me ___ to

par - a - dise, _ yeah, your sex takes me ___ to par - a - dise. _ And it

feel ___ like ___ I've been locked out of heav - en ___

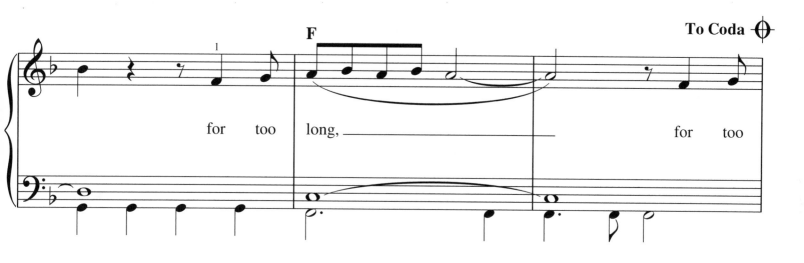

To Coda

for too long, ___ for too

long. ___

Oh, yeah, ___ yeah, yeah, yeah.

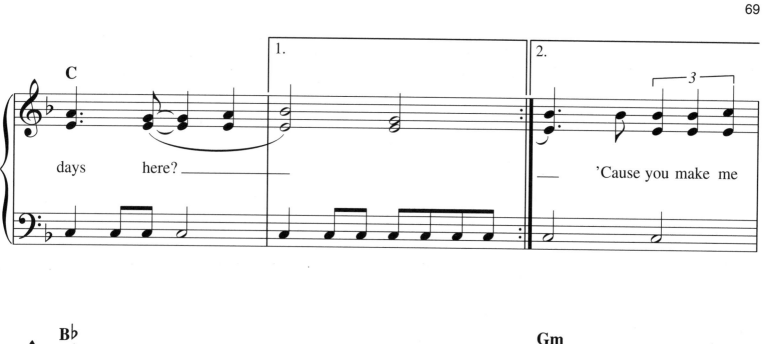

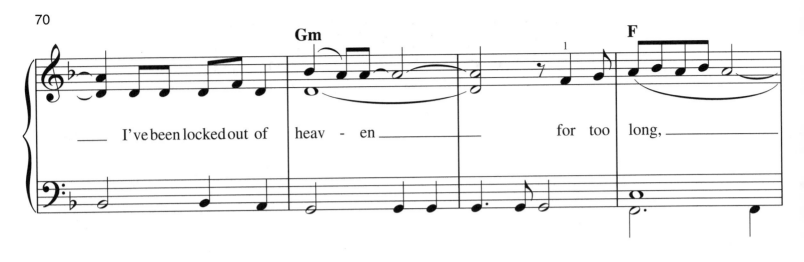

I've been locked out of heav - en _____ for too long, _____

_____ for too long.

Oh, yeah, _____ yeah, yeah, yeah.

Oh, yeah, _____ yeah, oh, yeah, _____ yeah, yeah, yeah.

WE ARE NEVER EVER GETTING BACK TOGETHER

Words and Music by TAYLOR SWIFT,
SHELLBACK and MAX MARTIN

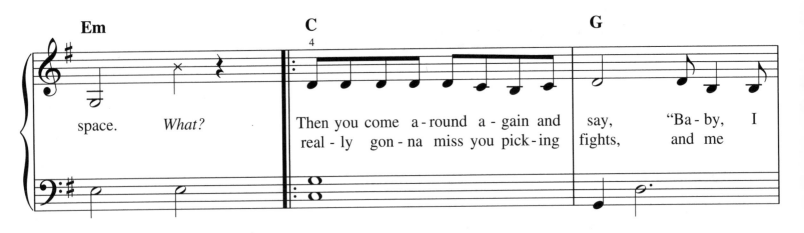

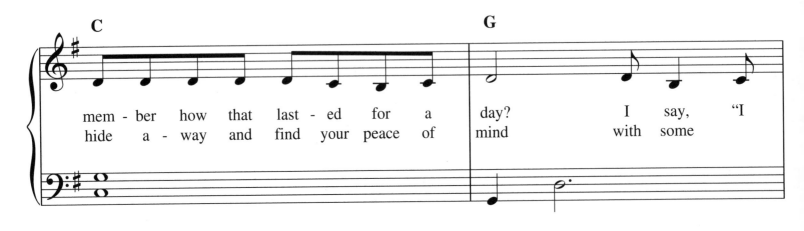

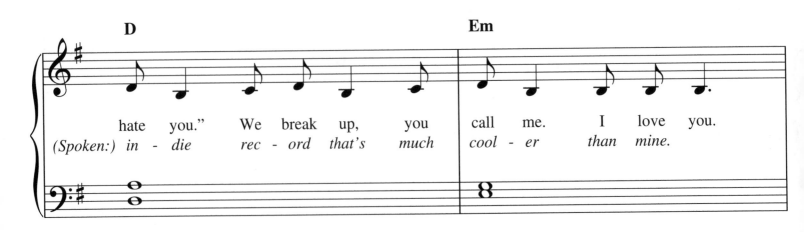

Ooh, ooh, ooh, ooh, we called it off a - gain
Ooh, ooh, ooh, ooh, you called me up a - gain

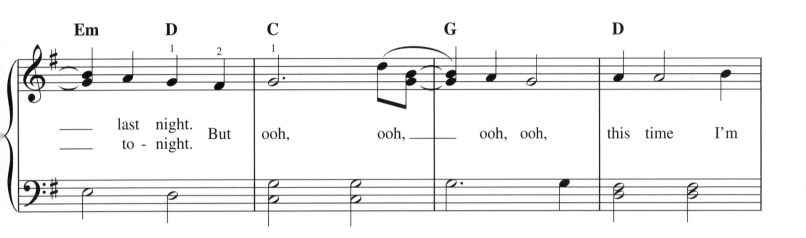

last night. But ooh, ooh, ooh, ooh, this time I'm
to - night.

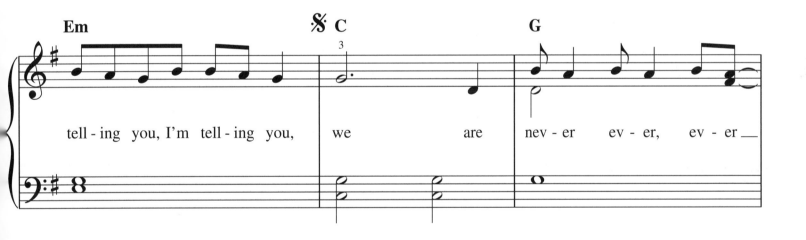

tell - ing you, I'm tell - ing you, we are nev - er ev - er, ev - er

get - ting back to - geth - er. We are nev - er ev - er, ev - er

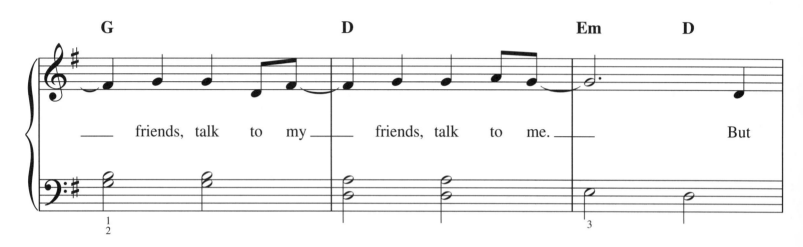

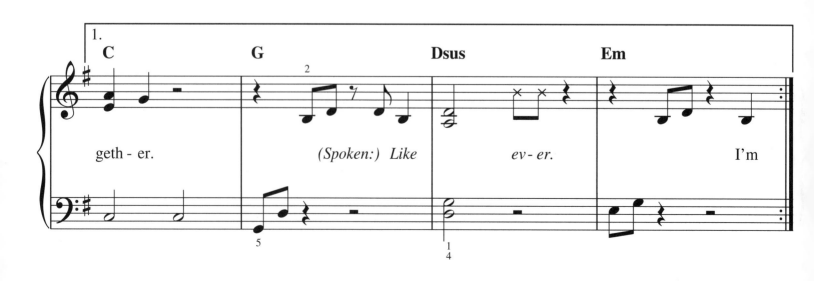

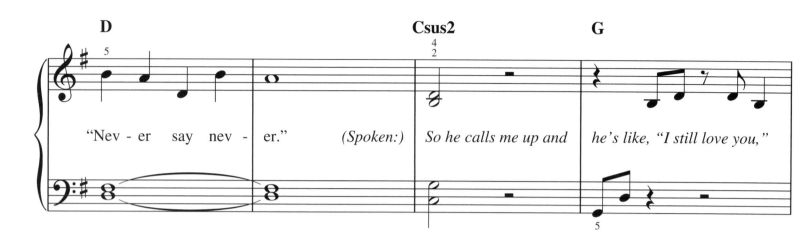

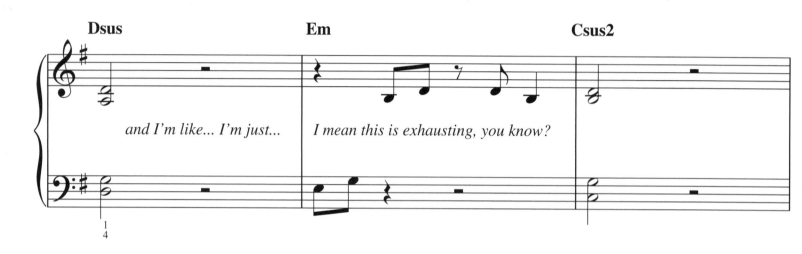

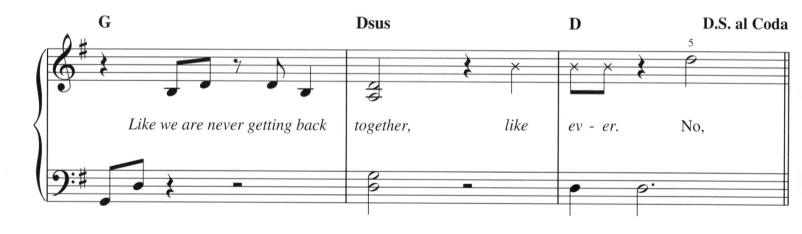

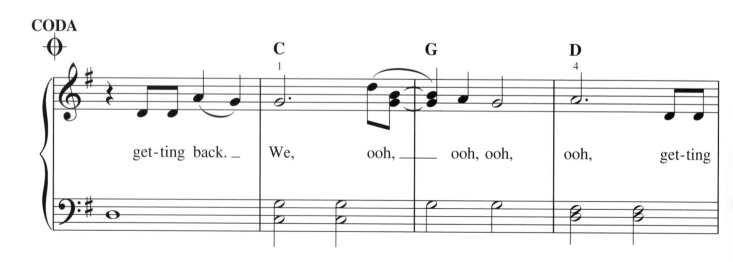

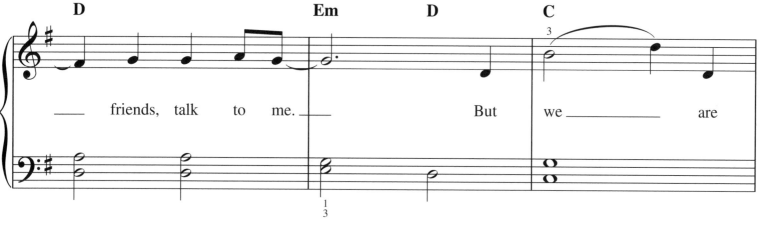

ONE MORE NIGHT

Words and Music by ADAM LEVINE,
JOHAN SCHUSTER and MAX MARTIN

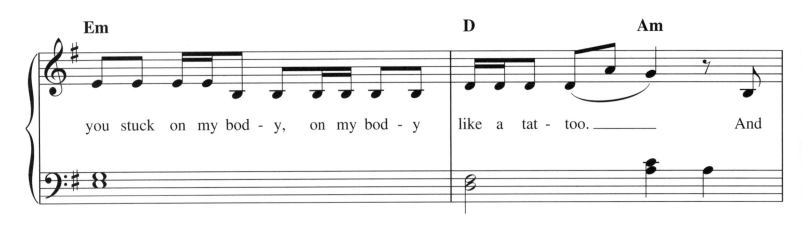

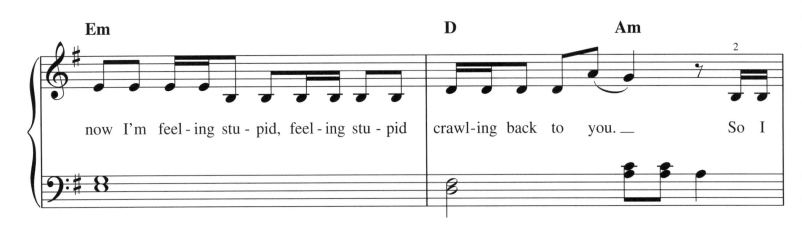

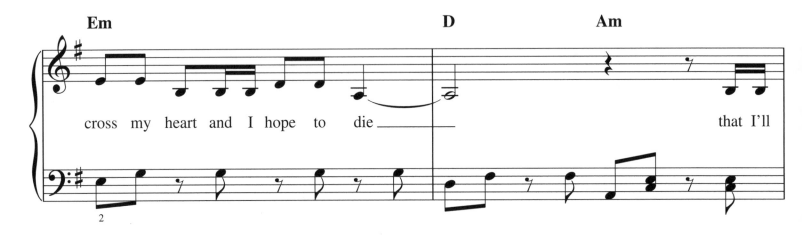

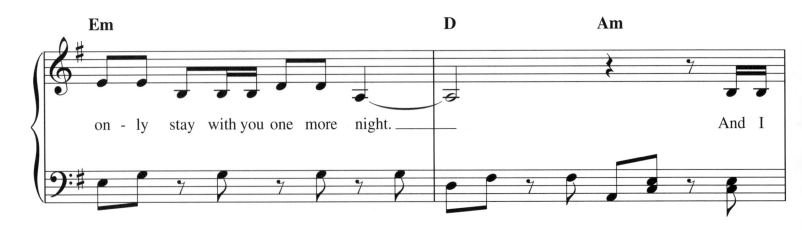

Oh, ba - by, there you go a - gain, there you go a - gain,

mak - ing me love you. ___ Yeah, I stopped us - ing my head, us - ing my head,

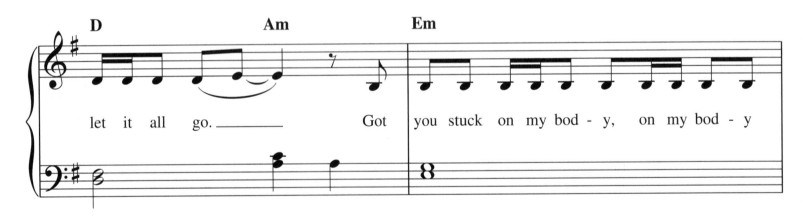

let it all go. _____ Got you stuck on my bod - y, on my bod - y

like a tat - too. _____ Yeah, _____ yeah, _____ yeah, yeah. __

SKYFALL
from the Motion Picture SKYFALL

Words and Music by ADELE ADKINS
and PAUL EPWORTH

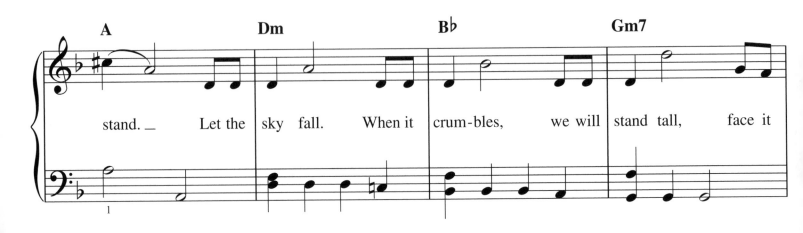

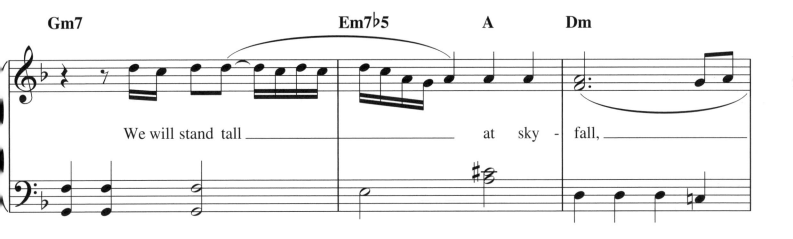

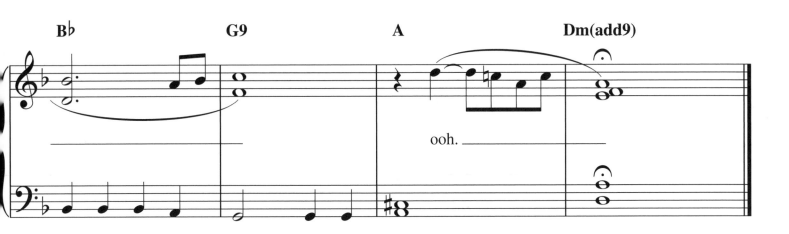

SOME NIGHTS

Words and Music by JEFF BHASKER,
ANDREW DOST, JACK ANTONOFF
and NATE RUESS

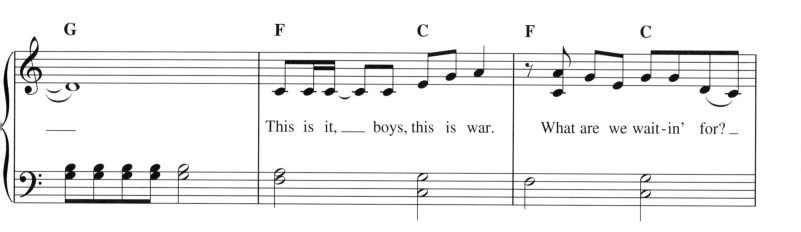

Why don't we break the rules al - read - y? I was

nev - er one __ to be-lieve the hype, __ save that for the black and white. I try

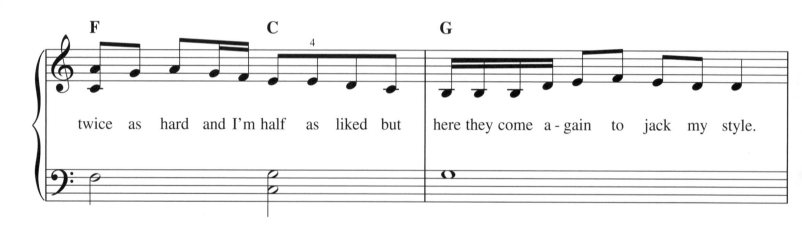

twice as hard and I'm half as liked but here they come a - gain to jack my style.

That's al - right; I found a mar-tyr in my bed to-night. She

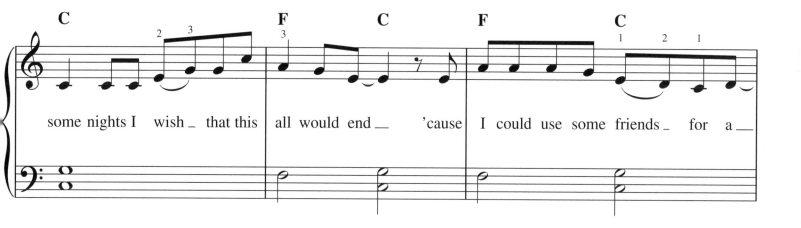

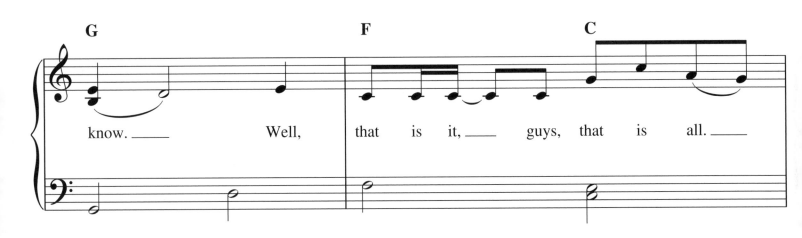

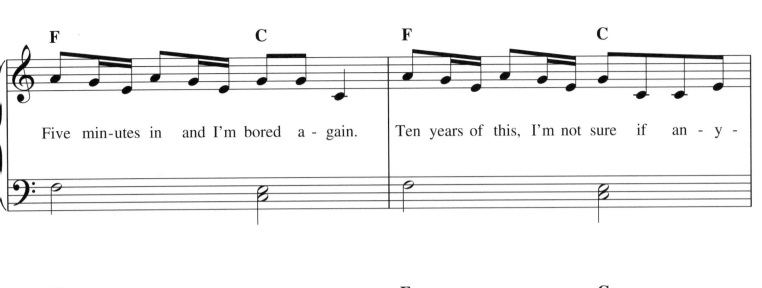

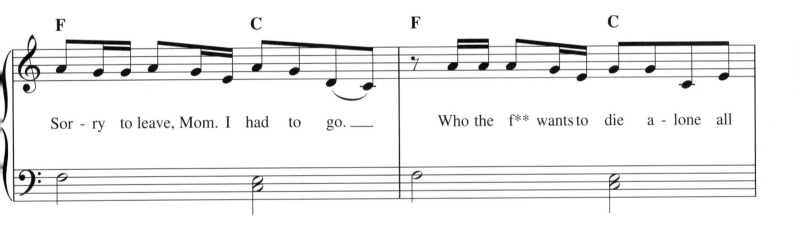

con that she call "love." _ And I look in - to my neph - ew's eyes. _

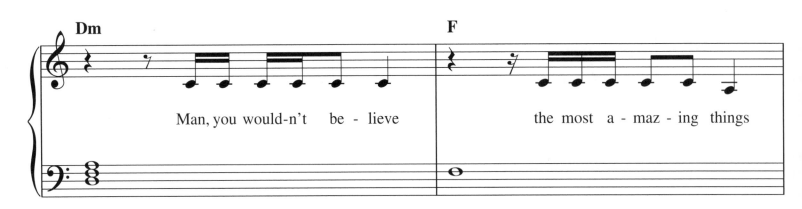

Man, you would-n't be - lieve the most a - maz - ing things

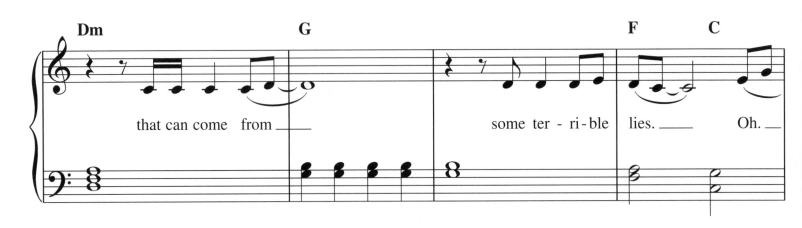

that can come from _ some ter - ri - ble lies. _ Oh. _

Oh. _

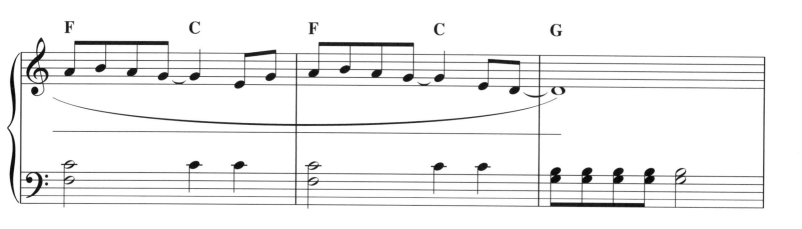

The oth-er night you would-n't be-lieve the dream I just had a-bout you and me.

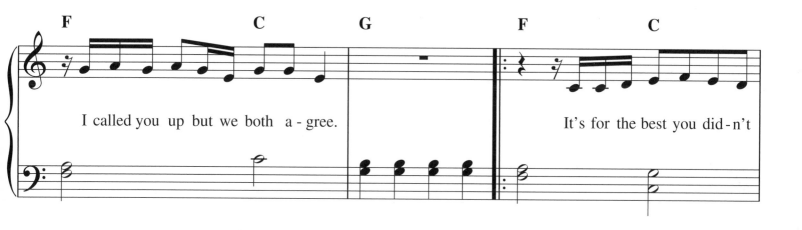

I called you up but we both a-gree. It's for the best you did-n't

lis-ten. ___ It's for the best we get our dis-tance, ___ oh.

TOO CLOSE

Words and Music by ALEX CLAIRE
and JIM DUGUID

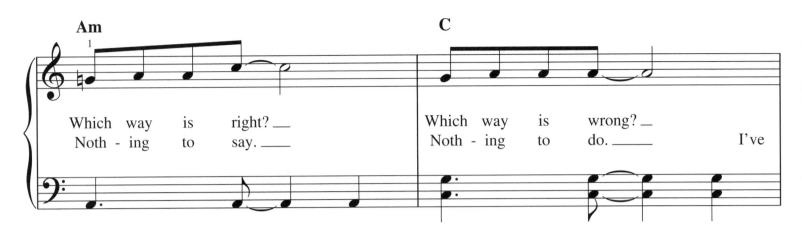

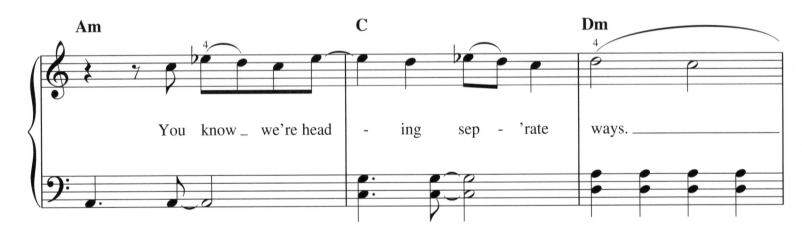

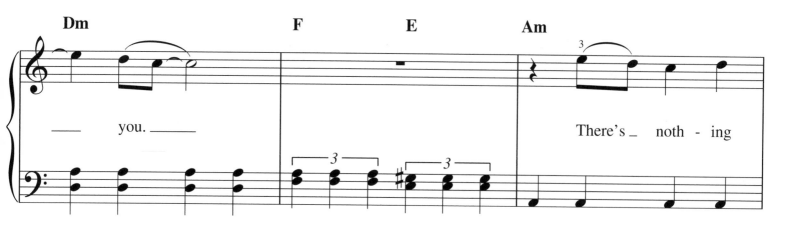

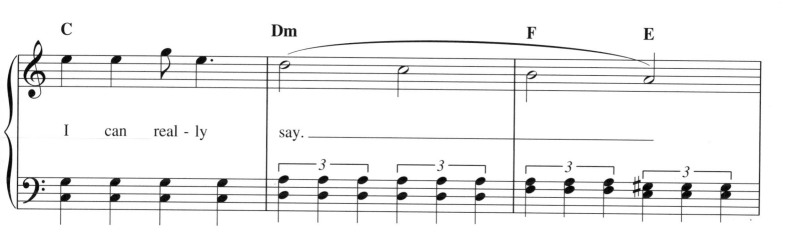

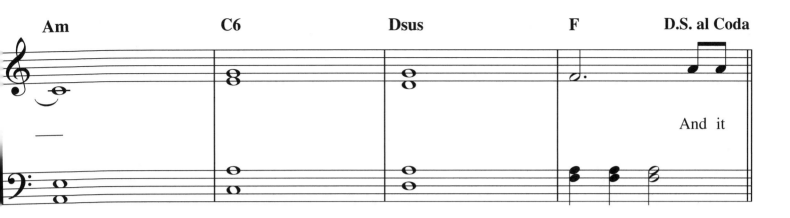

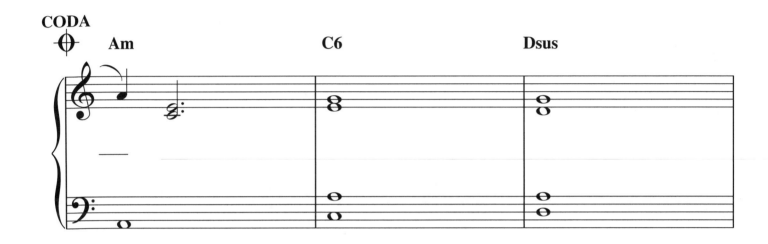

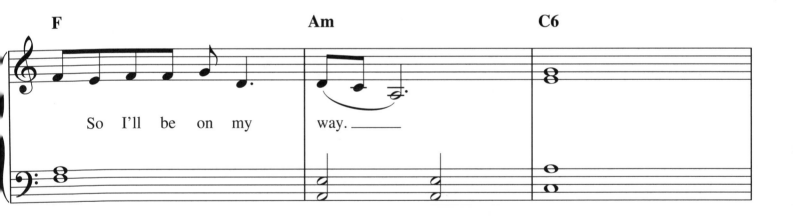

EASY PIANO CD PLAY-ALONGS
Orchestrated arrangements with you as the soloist!

This series lets you play along with great accompaniments to songs you know and love! Each book comes with a CD of complete professional performances and includes matching custom arrangements in easy piano format. With these books you can: Listen to complete professional performances of each of the songs; Play the easy piano arrangements along with the performances; Sing along with the recordings; Play the easy piano arrangements as solos, without the CD.

1. GREAT JAZZ STANDARDS
00310916 .... $14.95

2. FAVORITE CLASSICAL THEMES
00310921 .... $14.95

3. BROADWAY FAVORITES
00310915 .... $14.95

5. HIT POP/ROCK BALLADS
00310917 .... $14.95

6. LOVE SONG FAVORITES
00310918 .... $14.95

7. O HOLY NIGHT
00310920 .... $14.95

8. A CHRISTIAN WEDDING
00311104 .... $14.95

9. COUNTRY BALLADS
00311105 .... $14.95

10. MOVIE GREATS
00311106 .... $14.95

11. DISNEY BLOCKBUSTERS
00311107 .... $14.95

12. CHRISTMAS FAVORITES
00311257 .... $14.95

13. CHILDREN'S SONGS
00311258 .... $14.95

14. CHILDREN'S FAVORITES
00311259 .... $14.95

15. DISNEY'S BEST
00311260 .... $14.95

16. LENNON & McCARTNEY HITS
00311262 .... $14.95

17. HOLIDAY HITS
00311329 .... $14.95

18. HIGH SCHOOL MUSICAL
00311752 .... $16.99

20. ANDREW LLOYD WEBBER – FAVORITES
00311775 .... $14.99

21. GREAT CLASSICAL MELODIES
00311776 .... $14.99

22. ANDREW LLOYD WEBBER – HITS
00311785 .... $14.99

23. DISNEY CLASSICS
00311836 .... $14.99

24. LENNON & McCARTNEY FAVORITES
00311837 .... $14.99

26. WICKED
00311882 .... $16.99

27. THE SOUND OF MUSIC
00311897 .... $14.99

28. CHRISTMAS CAROLS
00311912 .... $14.99

29. CHARLIE BROWN CHRISTMAS
00311913 .... $14.99

30. GLEE
00312194 .... $14.99

Disney characters and artwork © Disney Enterprises, Inc.

PEANUTS © United Feature Syndicate, Inc.

Prices, contents and availability subject to change without notice.

FOR MORE INFORMATION, SEE YOUR LOCAL MUSIC DEALER, OR WRITE TO:

HAL•LEONARD® CORPORATION
7777 W. BLUEMOUND RD. P.O. BOX 13819 MILWAUKEE, WI 53213

www.halleonard.com

0812